Contents

KU-765-849

What is a monarchy?   4

Tapping tradition   6

Might makes right?   10

For king and country   14

Mixing it up   18

Making a monarchy work   22

Clash of interests   25

Changing times   29

Heirs to the throne   32

End of the line   36

Monarchy and the media   40

Looking ahead   44

Glossary   46

Books and websites   47

Index   48

What is a monarchy?

In a world of iPads and virtual reality it sometimes seems hard to believe that kings and queens still exist, except as part of a computer game or a dressing-up activity. Yet the truth is that nearly 50 countries still have a monarchy – the type of government that has a king or queen at its heart.

What is even more surprising is that many people living in those countries believe their system to be fair and just. The Dutch, for example, believe that theirs is one of the most forward-looking, tolerant societies in the world. Yet they live in a monarchy. Canadians live in a wide-open country that has the skyscrapers, big cars and glamour of its neighbour the United States. Yet the Canadian **head of state** is whoever sits on the throne more than 5,000 kilometres away in Britain.

Those countries, like most of the world's monarchies, have succeeded in introducing the best aspects of representative governments (such as fair elections and a **free press**) while preserving the sense of history and tradition that reassures many people living in monarchies. Even the monarchies that have done less to move into the modern era can claim to provide the right government for their people, for the same reasons of history and tradition.

Shared background

Like so many words used to define other types of government, the word monarchy comes from Greek. It derives from the Greek words *monos arkhein*, meaning 'one ruler'. Most monarchies were establised after a single ruler emerged from power struggles to rule over a nation.

Many monarchies have similar origins (even if the original power struggles were centuries ago). Today, though, there is no single

Systems of Government

MONARCHY

Sean Connolly

W

Windsor and Maidenhead

9580000062552

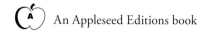 An Appleseed Editions book

Paperback edition, revised and updated 2017
First published in 2012 by Franklin Watts

© 2012 Appleseed Editions

Created by Appleseed Editions Ltd,
Well House, Friars Hill, Guestling,
East Sussex TN35 4ET

Designed by Hel James
Edited by Mary-Jane Wilkins
Picture research by Su Alexander

All rights reserved. No part of this publication may be reproduced, stored in a retrieval system
or transmitted in any form or by any means, electronic, mechanical, photocopying, recording
or otherwise, without prior permission of the publisher.

ISBN 978 1 4451 5345 2
Dewey Classification 321.8'7

A CIP catalogue for this book is available from the British Library.

Picture credits
Page 5 Getty Images; 7 Thinkstock; 9 Photos.com/Thinkstock; 10 MCT via Getty Images; 12 Getty
Images; 14 Dutourdumonde/Shutterstock; 16 Tim Graham/Getty Images; 18 Getty Images; 20 Tim
Graham/Getty Images; 23 Getty Images; 25 Photos.com/Thinkstock; 26 Tim Graham/Getty Images;
30 WireImage/Getty Images; 31 AFP/Getty Images; 32 Tim Graham/Getty Images; 34 & 36 AFP/
Getty Images; 38 Getty Images; 40 Lorna Roberts/Shutterstock.com; 43 AFP/Getty Images;
45 Tim Graham/Getty Images

Printed in China

Franklin Watts
An imprint of Hachette Children's Group
Part of The Watts Publishing Group
Carmelite House
50 Victoria Embankment
London EC4Y 0DZ

an Hachette UK Company
www.hachette.co.uk

www.franklinwatts.co.uk

blueprint for monarchies in the modern world. Each one has chosen – or been forced – to change in some way. In some modern societies, the monarch is elected. In others, the monarch stands apart from day-to-day politics as a sort of referee and national symbol. Each variation, however, tries to retain the sense of tradition that many find so important in a monarchy. This book examines how monarchies coexist with a fast-changing world. Could one of the oldest forms of government – which draws its strength from looking back – be the best one to look ahead into an unknown future?

The wedding of Prince William and Catherine Middleton in April 2011 captured the imagination of the British public. For many, this 'fairy tale' wedding offered escape from the economic bad news..

TIMELINE... TIMELINE... TIMELINE... TIMELINE... TIMELINE... TIMELINE...

2500   Gilgamesh becomes King of Uruk, in what is now Iraq   2100   Xia **Dynasty** begins in China

Tapping tradition

At the heart of any type of government is an exchange between political leaders and the people of a country. A **democracy** is an obvious example: the people choose their leaders by electing them. In return for being chosen, the political leaders agree to guide the country sensibly. The alternative is clear: if they don't live up to expectations, they are voted out of office.

It is harder to see the exchange in a monarchy, especially as the first monarchies rewarded the most powerful warriors with political power. Over the years, though, the number of such **absolute monarchies** (see page 11) has diminished; kings and queens, emperors and **emirs** have had to acknowledge the rights and wishes of their people. That acknowledgement forms part of the exchange that exists at the heart of monarchies today.

National heritage

Most people like to feel proud of their country, whether because of its sporting success, military victories, cultural history, or the character of its people. The desire to feel these strengths, which help define the country, runs deep in the national fabric. French people, for example, have celebrated their skills in cooking, fashion and coolness under pressure for centuries. Greeks are proud of their contribution to thinking, architecture and the arts. All these qualities make up a country's heritage.

Monarchies, and the age-old systems they represent, are an important feature in the heritage of many countries. Britain is one of them. Tourists come from all over the world to see Buckingham Palace, the Changing of the Guard and the treasures of the Tower of London. All are essential elements of the British monarchy. British people pay a great deal for this heritage, but that is where the exchange comes in.

In effect, British taxpayers feel that they provide the royal family with luxury, honour and some responsibilities; in exchange, the royal family provides taxpayers with a link to the past and a powerful sense of the nation's heritage. The (usually) unspoken addition to such sentiment might be: 'We also acknowledge that the pageantry and ceremonies attached to all this tradition have a healthy effect on our economy, and we feel that you contibute by attracting foreign visitors to our country.'

This view of monarchy is the most common in the twenty-first century. It would be foolish of a newly independent country to create a monarchy and expect people to obey or even respect it. The attraction of a monarchy is its links with the past. Most people who live in this

Centuries-old ceremonies, such as Trooping the Colour (above), underpin the monarchy's role in British society.

TIMELINE... TIMELINE... TIMELINE... TIMELINE... TIMELINE... TIMELINE...

1066　**Zhou Dynasty begins in China**　　1047　**Saul becomes first King of Israel**

kind of system today accept this state of affairs: they either pay little attention to the monarchy (because real power is held by elected leaders) or approve of having people set apart who act as national symbols.

Blurred boundaries

Most countries with monarchies must address a fundamental question: where does symbolism end and real power begin? Does the political system make it clear where those boundaries are? What would happen if a king or queen (or their representative) decided to enter the political battlefield? That is what many Australians believe occurred in their country in 1975 (see page 28).

Less dramatically, Prince Charles has been accused of meddling when he has expressed strong views on architecture, possibly influencing government decisions on which architects to employ and how British cities should look. Then again, it can be argued that monarchies have

HEAD OF STATE

Nearly every government of any type has a person who represents the state (or nation) in public affairs. The famous French leader Charles de Gaulle described that role as embodying 'the spirit of the nation'. France no longer has a monarchy, but the French elect a president to act as their head of state. That role in Britain and in other monarchies is held by the reigning monarch.

Defenders of monarchy like to point out that a royal head of state (as opposed to an elected one) is not linked to divisive politics. In their view, Queen Elizabeth is an effective head of state because she stands outside politics. Unlike elected political leaders, she has not had to make promises (or make enemies) to achieve her position. She was born to do the job, and can do it better than anyone else.

Opponents argue that being born to a job is no guarantee that someone can do that job well. Some might argue that although Elizabeth does a good job as queen, there is no guarantee that her son – or grandson – will do as good a job.

TIMELINE... TIMELINE... TIMELINE... TIMELINE... TIMELINE... TIMELINE

753 BCE Romulus (according to legend) becomes first Roman king

never been completely removed from the people. Britain's king and queen were welcome symbols of British spirit during London's darkest hours during the **Second World War**, so why should their grandson (Charles) have to stay out of the public eye? Britain's is not the only monarchy that needs to balance progress and tradition. Every king, queen, prince, emir, **sultan** – even the Pope – must be able to move with the times, while also symbolizing the past in some way.

LE ROY LOVIS XIV
PROCLAME LE DVC D'ANJOV
ROY D'ESPAGNE
LE 16 NOVEMBRE 1700

Louis XIV reigned over France for 72 years in the seventeenth and eighteenth century. By forcing noblemen to live in his lavish palace of Versailles, Louis cleverly managed to keep an eye on potential threats to his power.

TIMELINE... TIMELINE... TIMELINE... TIMELINE... TIMELINE... TIMELINE...

660 Japanese monarchy founded, the world's oldest existing monarchy

Might makes right?

One drawback of any elected government is
that it can take a long time to make or change laws.
When US president Barack Obama was elected in 2008,
he promised to reform the country's medical system so
that more Americans would receive medical insurance.
His opponents fought every attempt to make those
changes, so the idea was debated over and over again
in the US **Congress**.

TIMELINE... TIMELINE... TIMELINE... TIMELINE... TIMELINE... TIMELINE

587 BCE   Babylonian King Nebuchadnezzar II destroys Jerusalem and sends thousands of Jews into exile

Eventually the **bill** was passed, but it had taken nearly fifteen months to reach that point. By the time it was passed, Obama and his supporters in Congress had had to agree to a number of **compromises** that severely limited the original idea. Nobody was really happy with this. Keen supporters of reform regretted the way in which Obama had been forced to give ground on so many issues. Opponents of reform wondered why Congress had spent so much time on the issue when it had more important matters to debate.

Opponents of President Obama's health care proposals protest angrily in Washington. Supporters of monarchies argue that a king or queen can help soothe such national divisions and help people to find common ground.

What I say goes

Imagine how attractive it would be for leaders to be able to say: 'From tomorrow, we drive on the right' or 'I've heard enough – send that troublemaker to jail'. That is the sort of power an absolute monarch has. Most European monarchies began with a ruler claiming power, but throughout the Middle Ages influential **nobles** could gang together and try to depose a king if they disagreed with his leadership.

European monarchs gained more power during the seventeenth and eighteenth centuries, largely because nations became more centralized and so were more easily controlled by one person. Monarchs also gained power by being able to raise taxes with less interference from the nobles. King Louis XIV of France summed up his position with two memorable phrases: '*une foi, une loi, un roi*' (one faith, one law, one king) and '*l'etat, c'est moi*' (the state is me). In this view of absolute monarchy, the king (or queen) is the element that holds the country together.

By the mid-eighteenth century democratic ideas were spreading across Europe and most monarchies had to give away powers or face outright **revolution**. The seeds of the modern British system of **constitutional monarchy** (see pages 16-17) were sown at this time, with the reigning monarch assuming more of a symbolic role. Other monarchies held on to absolute power, even into the twentieth century. The Russian **tsar** continued to take many important government decisions right up to the time of the Russian Revolution in 1917. The Japanese emperor (see panel) was theoretically in charge of the branches of government – and even the state religion – until 1947.

TIMELINE... TIMELINE... TIMELINE... TIMELINE... TIMELINE... TIMELINE...

509 Roman monarchy abolished   **323** Alexander the Great dies and his empire is split into three parts

Modern examples

Today, only six countries – mostly small ones – can claim to be absolute monarchies, in which the monarch is head of both state and government: they are Brunei, Oman, Qatar, Saudi Arabia, Swaziland and Vatican City. Pro-democracy elements have called for change – and have occasionally faced violent reaction from the police – in four of those countries. The only exceptions are Vatican City, where most of the population is involved with the headquarters of the Catholic Church, and Brunei, whose small population is relatively well off because of the country's oil wealth.

Japan's Emperor Hirohito inspects bomb damage in Tokyo caused by an American bombing raid in October 1943.

TIMELINE... TIMELINE... TIMELINE... TIMELINE... TIMELINE... TIMELINE...

221 BCE   **Qin Dynasty begins in China**   206   **Han Dynasty begins in China**

'AFTER PONDERING DEEPLY...'

The term for the Japanese monarch is emperor, although Japan did not have an empire for much of its history. It only began to expand greatly when it invaded China and much of south-east Asia in the 1930s, helping to trigger the Second World War. Throughout the war, Japanese soldiers and ordinary people were prepared to die for their emperor, who was considered almost a god.

After the Americans dropped two massively destructive atomic bombs on Japanese cities in August 1945, it became clear that Japan would be defeated, no matter what it did. Surrender was the only alternative, but that went against the Japanese code of honour.

It was Emperor Hirohito who made the decision to surrender, a decision he announced to the Japanese people on the radio on 15 August 1945: 'To our good and loyal subjects: after pondering deeply the general trends of the world and the actual conditions obtaining to our empire today, we have decided to effect a settlement of the present situation by resorting to an extraordinary measure. We have ordered our government to communicate to the governments of the United States, Great Britain, China and the Soviet Union that our empire accepts the provisions of their joint declaration.' (The provisions called for Japan's surrender.)

He chose not to use the word 'surrender' in that opening and went on to say that Japan had only entered the war to protect itself. With the enemy using a cruel new weapon he said: 'Should we continue to fight, it would not only result in an ultimate collapse and [destruction] of the Japanese nation, but also it would lead to the total extinction of human civilization.'

The emperor had cleverly protected Japan's cherished sense of honour. According to him, Japan had entered the war in self-defence and had willingly ended it to protect human civilization. It is hard to imagine an elected leader getting away with those words – and being believed by his people.

For king and country

We can learn a lot about how countries see themselves by listening to their national anthems. Many nations sing proudly of how they rid themselves of monarchies at some point in their history and how the governments which replaced those monarchies – according to the anthems – promote freedom and reflect the wishes of the people.

Argentina, ruled by the Spanish monarchy for centuries, celebrates its independence with the words:
'Mortals! Hear the sacred cry:
Freedom! Freedom! Freedom!'

France's violent revolution overthrew its monarchy. Then, according to its national anthem, conservative European countries (including Great Britain) ganged up on France and tried to snuff out its new freedom:
'Arise children of the fatherland
The day of glory has arrived
Against us tyranny's
Bloody **standard** is raised.'

The German anthem is less extreme but still celebrates 'Unity and justice and freedom for the German fatherland.'

Even countries that have got rid of their monarchies need symbols. The French use an idealized image of French womanhood, nicknamed Marianne, as a symbol of their nation. Instead of a crown, she wears the floppy cap that was popular during the French Revolution in the late eighteenth century.

Compare all those sentiments with the words of the British national anthem:
'Send her victorious,
Happy and glorious,
Long to reign over us:
God save the Queen.'

Or the Japanese anthem:
'May thy peaceful reign last long!
May it last for thousands of years.'

Neither the British nor the Japanese anthem mentions justice, freedom, equality or liberty. Instead they sing the praises of loyalty and tradition. The basis of the loyalty and tradition is the monarchy in each case. But do the British and Japanese consider themselves less free, or more oppressed than the Argentines, French and Germans?

Subjects or citizens?

Another way of looking at this issue is to see that the two systems aim for the same target – a just and fair society – but take different routes. One route is typified by the French and American systems. Both those countries rejected monarchy in the eighteenth century and produced documents stating how their governments would operate.

TIMELINE... TIMELINE... TIMELINE... TIMELINE... TIMELINE... TIMELINE...

Lords gather at the State Opening of Britain's Parliament. Can unelected noblemen really play a part in a modern democracy?

The US Constitution, which was adopted in 1787, is still the supreme law of the United States. Two years later, about a month after their revolution had begun, the French adopted the *Declaration of the Rights of Man and of the **Citizen***. Like the American document, it announced that all people had basic rights, and that governments could be chosen by those people to protect their rights.

Both these countries, and many others that followed their example, believed that a nation's people were all equal in the eyes of the law. No one was superior, or guaranteed special powers. The term 'citizen' emphasized that. Although the French brought back the monarchy briefly in the nineteenth century, the idea of citizenship still lies at the heart of the French political system.

TIMELINE... TIMELINE... TIMELINE... TIMELINE... TIMELINE... TIMELINE..

843 CE   **Kingdom of France established**   843   **Kenneth MacAlpine becomes first King of (a united) Scotland**

The British people at that time, on the other hand, were proud to consider themselves subjects rather than citizens. They heard about the violence surrounding the French Revolution – up to 40,000 French 'free citizens' lost their heads on the guillotine – and drew comfort from their own secure monarchy.

Constitutional monarchy

The British political system, unlike those in the United States and France, has no written constitution. Instead, the laws passed by Parliament and the decisions taken by British judges form what is often called an unwritten constitution. The British monarchy has evolved within such a system, with parliamentary bills or legal judgements edging it in new directions.

The result is that the United Kingdom has a system called a constitutional monarchy. A constitutional monarchy is often seen as the opposite of an absolute monarchy. Most monarchies today are constitutional. The unelected head of state retains symbolic power, but in reality is governed by the wishes of the elected political leaders. Supporters of such systems argue that they offer the best of all worlds: the ordinary voters still choose leaders who have real power, while the monarchy provides the tradition and heritage that many democracies lack.

THE VOTING BOOTH

Peaceful coexistence?

Few people would argue that the reigning British monarch has real political power in the twenty-first century. But many opponents of the system argue that having an unelected head of state at the top of the political system affects the way people view the entire system. For example, in their view, it justifies having an unelected section of the real political system (the House of Lords).

Can monarchy and democracy really coexist, or will there always be a clash if some people are born into positions of power or honour?

TIMELINE... TIMELINE... TIMELINE... TIMELINE... TIMELINE... TIMELINE...

924   Athelstan becomes King of England – accepted by many historians as the first

Mixing it up

There is no blueprint for the way monarchies operate. Some follow the British pattern of constitutional monarchy, with a largely symbolic monarch acting as head of state and succeeding (taking over from) the previous monarch through **heredity**. Others elect their monarch or use different methods of royal succession. Some newly independent countries choose to maintain historical ties with other monarchies through associations such as the **Commonwealth of Nations**.

The Commonwealth

Driving across the border from the United States to Canada, visitors might find it hard to spot any differences between the two countries. The cars look the same, the people sound the same, and there is a similar mix of forest and farmland, suburb and high-rise city skylines. But as soon as they stop to buy something, they will notice something very different.

Most Canadian coins are the same size and are of similar value to their American counterparts, but one side of Canadian coins depicts Queen Elizabeth II of Great Britain. The British no longer rule Canada as they once did. Canada is an independent country, and makes its own

A spectacular closing ceremony brings to an end the 2010 Commonwealth Games in India. The games are run along the lines of the Olympic Games, and bring together teams from the 54 member nations of the Commonwealth.

ELECTING A KING?

Queen Elizabeth II inherited the British throne when her father, King George VI, died in 1952. The British succession is based on heredity, which means that the heir to the throne is ready to become king or queen as soon as the reigning monarch dies. The phrase 'The king is dead; long live the king!' sums up the advantage of a hereditary monarchy. The title passes smoothly and without disagreement from one person to another.

Heredity is not the only type of royal succession, though. Many monarchies have used elections to decide on a new ruler. Assemblies in ancient Rome chose each new king (before Rome became a republic in 509 BCE). A group of nobles, called prince-electors, chose the **Holy Roman Emperor** throughout much of the Middle Ages.

There are a few modern elected monarchies. Hereditary rulers of the nine Malay states elect a supreme head of state for a five-year term. The Royal Council of the Throne (made up of nobles with royal blood) chooses Cambodia's king for a life term. The **College of Cardinals** elects a successor when a pope dies.

TIMELINE... TIMELINE... TIMELINE... TIMELINE... TIMELINE... TIMELINE...

and is crowned King of England   1139   Kingdom of Portugal established

decisions on national and international matters, but it does retain an important connection with Great Britain, which explains the image of the British monarch on its money.

The Commonwealth of Nations (Commonwealth for short) is a voluntary group of 54 independent nations that share values of freedom, justice and cooperation. Most of the countries have historical ties with Great Britain and in many cases were British colonies at one time. Canada is part of a smaller group of 16 nations called Commonwealth realms (countries which recognize the reigning British monarch as their head of state). This means that among her many titles, Elizabeth II is Queen of Canada.

Most Commonwealth realms also have elected governments similar to the British one, and bills in Commonwealth realms need royal approval in the same way as bills passed in the British Parliament before they become law (see page 24). The monarch's representative, or **governor-general**, does the approving.

TIMELINE... TIMELINE... TIMELINE... TIMELINE... TIMELINE... TIMELINE...

1215 CE **King John signs Magna Carta, limiting powers of the English monarch**

AN AUSTRALIAN REPUBLIC?

The Commonwealth realm with the most vocal anti-monarchy movement is Australia. Many Australians trace their ancestry to Ireland and resent the role Britain has played there over the years. Australia has a strong trade union movement, which tends to oppose the 'stuffiness' of royalty in general. More recently, Australians have begun to think of themselves as part of the Asian sphere, rather than linked to much more distant Britain.

Most Australians who oppose the monarchy are republicans – they want Australia to be a **republic** (like France or the United States) with an elected head of state. Australia held a **referendum** in 1999, to find out whether voters wanted it to become a republic. The proposal to change the existing system failed, with 55 per cent of voters choosing to stick with the monarchy. Since then, the republican movement has gained some support, but not much. A poll in August 2010 found that 48 per cent of Australians wanted to keep the monarchy, while 44 per cent preferred a republican system.

Anti-monarchy protesters use their national holiday, Australia Day, to call for a republic to replace Australia's ties with the British monarchy.

VOICE OF THE PEOPLE

RESPECT FOR BETTY WINDSOR
When Queensland resident James MacPherson added his comments to a blog about Australia's monarchy, he came down on the side of a republic. However, he mixes this preference with some earthy admiration for the present British (and Australian) monarch, Queen Elizabeth II: 'I hope that Australia becomes a republic, with a head of state elected by the people. I have the greatest respect for Betty Windsor [Queen Elizabeth, whose surname is technically Windsor] and the job that she has done as our monarch – Queen of Australia – but I despise and detest the concept of hereditary privilege, and I loathe the royal family.'

TIMELINE... TIMELINE... TIMELINE... TIMELINE... TIMELINE... TIMELINE...

1271   Yuan Dynasty (founded by Mongol leader Kublai Khan) begins in China

Making a monarchy work

Very few monarchies have come into being since the seventeenth century. Some new monarchies have been formed partly by outside forces, or as a result of wider political needs. Belgium became independent in 1830 at a time when major European powers were trying to prevent any one country from becoming too powerful (as France had become under **Napoleon**). Yugoslavia was formed in 1918 by merging a number of states that had been part of the **Austro-Hungarian Empire**, which was broken up at the end of the **First World War**.

Both Belgium and Yugoslavia chose to follow the example of Great Britain by becoming constitutional monarchies. The choice made sense: supporters of monarchies argue that the head of state (the monarch) stands above the arguing of political parties or nationalities that make up the nation. Queen Elizabeth II, for example, is not just monarch of the English, but of the Welsh, Scots and some Irish (not to mention Australians, Canadians, New Zealanders and others living in the Commonwealth realms).

Delicate balance
Other monarchies have taken a thousand years or more to arrive at the system that Belgium and Yugoslavia chose to adopt. Those new arrivals could not claim centuries of tradition, but their founders saw the value of having a monarch as a symbol of political neutrality at the head of a government.

In Britain, no one would even begin to imagine which political party the queen supports, although she outlines forthcoming

political plans in the **Queen's Speech** every year. The fact that her speech is written by members of the ruling government (whichever political party has a **majority** in Parliament) shows exactly who makes the decisions that affect Britain. However, all the work of those elected officials – in Parliament and in government generally – is technically unofficial until the monarch agrees to it.

The accompanying chart shows exactly how government plans (called bills) pass through Parliament before eventually becoming law. This process shows the workings of a constitutional monarchy. With very few exceptions, every modern monarch deals with a similar combination of 'hands-off' (for the nitty gritty of creating laws) and 'hands-on' (for approving them).

Indonesian President Susilo Bambang addresses senators and members of the Australian parliament in March 2010 during an official visit. Australian anti-monarchists feel that an Australian republic would be better placed to trade with its Asian neighbours.

TIMELINE... TIMELINE... TIMELINE... TIMELINE... TIMELINE... TIMELINE...

1368   **Ming Dynasty begins in China**   1375   **Acamapichtli becomes first Aztec ruler**

A BILL BECOMES LAW IN BRITAIN

House of Commons

First reading A bill is introduced, to be discussed at an agreed second date.

Second reading A minister introduces the bill and there is a debate and vote on whether to move on to further stages.

Committee stage A small cross-party committee (15–50 members) is formed to discuss the bill in detail.

Report stage The bill is reprinted, taking into account any suggested changes (amendments).

Third reading The last chance for the Commons to vote on whether the bill should proceed further. If they vote yes, the bill goes to the House of Lords.

House of Lords

First reading The bill approved by the Commons is introduced, to be discussed at an agreed second date.

Second reading The bill is discussed, but the Lords has far less scope for amendments than the Commons.

Report stage Only if considered necessary.

Third reading The final discussion and vote. If they vote yes, the bill only awaits the final stage.

Royal Assent

The monarch once signed each bill personally. Now the queen (or king) appoints special lords as Royal Commissioners to announce that Royal Assent has been granted. Only then does the bill become law.

Commonwealth countries have similar systems within their parliaments. In these countries, the governor-general (representing the British monarchy) provides the Royal Assent.

Clash of interests

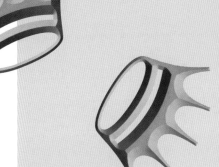

The words of the French national anthem make it clear that kings and queens are 'tyrants' and cannot be trusted. Their supporters are no better:

'Tremble, tyrants and traitors
The shame of all good men
Tremble! Your **parricidal** schemes
Will receive their just reward'

Those heated words no doubt suited the turbulent period of the French Revolution, and they echoed across much of Europe and beyond. Many people believed that the rulers who inherited their position (rather than being elected to it) would always behave selfishly and cruelly. The only solution – and the one chosen by the revolutionary French government – was to execute monarchs and get rid of the old system.

King Louis XVI is executed at the guillotine in Paris on 21 January 1793. From that point on, there was no turning back for the French revolutionaries.

Prince Charles visits Poundbury, a new town built in his preferred architectural style and on his own land.

Beheading was one way of resolving clashes between monarchs and their subjects, but it is hardly a fitting twenty-first century solution. How do today's monarchies deal with disagreements between a monarch and his or her country?

Checks and balances

The short answer to that question is that monarchs know better than to upset the people. In most constitutional monarchies, the heads of state receive much of their income from those very people, in grants and allowances that are decided by elected politicians. They are probably wealthy landowners in their own right (Prince Charles, for example, earns millions of pounds every year from his estates in Cornwall), but they depend on taxpayers for much of their income.

TIMELINE... TIMELINE... TIMELINE... TIMELINE... TIMELINE... TIMELINE...

1521 CE   Aztec Empire crushed by the Spanish   1533   Atahualpa, last Inca emperor, executed by Spanish

MONSTROUS CARBUNCLE

Queen Elizabeth II is noted for her calm, correct behaviour. She rarely shows emotion and has never been linked to a scandal that might trigger controversy. Her eldest son (and heir) Prince Charles, has been more forthright in expressing his opinions – and has been criticized as a result.

The prince has generated debate after publicly stating his opinions on medicine, farming and the teaching of English in schools. Perhaps his most famous public statements concern architecture. In 1984, he criticized plans to build a modern extension to the National Gallery, calling the proposed extension 'a monstrous **carbuncle** on the face of a much-loved and elegant friend'.

The comment sparked a fierce debate about the merits of modern versus old-fashioned architecture, but it went further than that. The prince's influence meant that other modern plans were quietly abandoned and many architects' careers suffered as a result. Some architects remain bitter about Prince Charles's comments decades later.

Leading architecture critic Rowan Moore, writing in the London *Evening Standard* in 2009, summed up their bitterness: 'The unelected prince, with a limited knowledge of architecture and planning and no accountability, became an unofficial additional organ of the planning system.'

As well as her personal income from property and investments (not funded by the public), the queen receives money from these publicly funded sources:
- grant-in-aid for the upkeep of royal palaces;
- the Privy Purse for official spending;
- the **Civil List** (which also funds other members of the **royal household**).

TIMELINE... TIMELINE... TIMELINE... TIMELINE... TIMELINE... TIMELINE...

1581   Dutch monarchy founded   1603   English and Scottish kingdoms united under one throne

Each of these categories has been criticized at one time or another because of the amounts of money involved, or because of negative reactions to the behaviour of the royal family. Scandals involving present or former members of the royal family can trigger a public outcry about spending millions each year on them. As a rule, the Civil List triggers the most public disapproval, especially when economic times are difficult for most people. The result of this complicated system of payments and allowances is that the royal family must not provoke disapproval.

A Commonwealth crisis

In late 1975, Australia's leading politicians were bitterly opposed on a number of issues including national borrowing, the appointment of ambassadors and the calling of elections. Prime minister Gough Whitlam of the Labor Party was determined to hold on to power because he had the support of the country's House of Representatives (the lower house of the parliament). Opposition leader Malcolm Fraser of the Liberal Party used his party's majority in the Senate (the upper house) to block bills which allowed tax money to be spent.

Whitlam decided to call for a half-Senate election, believing that the result would allow bills to pass through the Senate again. On 11 November 1975 he went to the governor-general, Sir John Kerr, to announce this intention. Usually such an announcement would be a formality, to be immediately approved by the queen's representative. Instead, the governor-general dismissed Whitlam and replaced him with Fraser. A general election was called on 13 December, which Fraser's Liberal Party won.

Sir John Kerr believed that his actions were the only way to solve the problem and to produce a strong decisive government. Many Australians, however, believed that he went well beyond his official role in dismissing an elected government. What do you think?

TIMELINE... TIMELINE... TIMELINE... TIMELINE... TIMELINE... TIMELINE...

1644 CE   Qing Dynasty begins in China   1649   King Charles I executed, ending English monarchy

Changing times

Centuries ago, monarchies were the most common form of government in Europe and beyond. Everyone, from the monarch to the poorest farm worker, knew his or her place. Today, the whole idea of monarchy is changing, which leads to all sorts of questions.

• What place do monarchies have in the twenty-first century?

• Are monarchies out of step with the modern world?

• Does a system of kings and queens, princes and princesses, exist simply to attract tourists to palaces and royal events?

• Might reigning monarchs have more than a symbolic role?

Most monarchies have managed to find answers to those questions that suit the needs and attitudes of their nation. The British expect their royal family to be formal, adding a traditional presence to ceremonies at home and state trips to foreign countries. The British royal family has become more open about its wealth and earnings – especially since economic times have become harder – but it has had to learn from public relations blunders (notably a misguided appearance by some members in a slapstick television game show in 1987) and the funeral of Diana, Princess of Wales, in 1997 (see Voice of the People).

The British monarchy represents a formal approach, while the monarchies of Scandinavia, the Netherlands and Belgium are examples of comparatively informal monarchies. Those nations expect their royal families to be part of wider society, rather than seeming to stand above it. People sometimes use the term 'bicycle monarchies' to describe those royal families. The phrase originated with Dutch Queen Juliana's habit of making unscheduled bike rides through the streets of Amsterdam.

Beyond tradition and pageantry

Now monarchs have mainly symbolic roles in today's constitutional monarchies, it is easy to dismiss them as being simply decorative. At best, they play a politically neutral, unthreatening role as head of state.

TIMELINE... TIMELINE... TIMELINE... TIMELINE... TIMELINE... TIMELINE...

1660   King Charles II crowned, restoring English monarchy

VOICE OF THE PEOPLE

Prince Charles, with his sons William and Harry, inspect the masses of flowers people left after the death of the young princes' mother, Diana, in August 1997.

THE PEOPLE'S PRINCESS

Diana, Princess of Wales, married Prince Charles in 1981, but the couple divorced in 1996. Diana was young and attractive and sometimes risked her life in her charity work. She seemed to breathe new life into the British monarchy. She remained popular after the divorce and the world was stunned when she died in a car accident in August 1997.

People displayed their grief openly and publicly in ways not usually associated with British reserve, yet the royal family seemed more removed from the public than usual in the days before her funeral. As the Independent *newspaper reported at the time, 'If only the royals dared weep with the people.'*

Tony Blair, prime minister at the time, was more in tune with public opinion, even finding a title for Diana (the people's princess) that captured the mood: 'People everywhere, not just here in Britain, kept faith with Princess Diana. They liked her, they loved her, they regarded her as one of the people. She was the People's Princess and that is how she will stay, how she will remain in our hearts and our memories for ever.'

Even in the twenty-first century, some monarchs have played an important part in preserving political calm. Belgium's monarchy, like the country itself, is less than 200 years old but the country faces serious divisions between its French-speaking (Walloon) population and its Flemish (Dutch) speakers. Tensions between these groups sometimes threaten to tear the country apart, and King Albert II has arranged many meetings between the two groups to help rebuild unity.

In Thailand, pro-democracy protesters, known as red shirts, clashed with police and soldiers in early 2010. King Bumiphol, who had the respect of both sides, helped cool the tension and avert civil war. The army seized power in 2014, and the king approved changes to the constitution to give the military more powers. Democratic elections were promised, but progress in that direction slowed, leaving many Thais disillusioned.

A Thai Red Shirt protest rocks Bangkok in March 2010. Many observers credit the country's king with preventing an all-out civil war.

TIMELINE... TIMELINE... TIMELINE... TIMELINE... TIMELINE... TIMELINE...

1707 CE   **Act of Union unites English and Scottish kingdoms**

Heirs to the throne

British prime minister David Cameron became leader of the Conservative Party in 2005, only four years after being elected to Parliament for the first time. Barack Obama, elected US president in 2008, had been a US senator since only 2004 and had served in the Illinois senate for seven years before that. They led their countries for six and eight years respectively, despite claims from many that they lacked experience.

TIMELINE... TIMELINE... TIMELINE... TIMELINE... TIMELINE... TIMELINE...

1792 CE   Execution of King Louis XVI ends the French monarchy

Are public attitudes different towards those who are born into, rather than elected, to leadership roles? The notion of job training is one area where the monarchy scores highly. While many people disagree with minor royals being given hand-outs from taxpayers' money, fewer people criticize the money spent on those likely to inherit the throne.

In some ways, being a royal is like being born in a bygone era, when sons and daughters knew from childhood how they would spend their adult lives – doing what their parents did. A prince can imagine being king in the same way that a coal miner's son could expect to work down the mines or a maid's daughter might follow in her mother's footsteps.

Prince Charles (left), with his sons William (right) and Harry, take part in a game of polo, a sport that is also known as 'the sport of kings'.

MEETING THE PEOPLE

Most Russians agree that Peter the Great (1672–1725) was their finest tsar. Standing nearly two metres tall, he towered over those around him and had a powerful personality. He built a modern new capital, Saint Petersburg, and reorganized many aspects of Russian society and government. As a young man, he travelled across Europe, staying in Germany, the Netherlands and England as he learned about shipbuilding, navies, architecture and many other subjects.

Since Peter's time, royal families have tried to find the best way to occupy heirs to the throne. Few have been as ambitious as Peter, who apparently travelled in secret. Most princes become associated with one of the armed forces: in Britain Prince William and Prince Harry have been given high-profile military training, for example. Their father, Prince Charles, trained in the air force and navy, but also became the first member of the British royal family to study for a university degree, which he was awarded by Cambridge University in 1970.

TIMELINE... TIMELINE... TIMELINE... TIMELINE... TIMELINE... TIMELINE...

1801   United Kingdom of Great Britain and Ireland formed

The 'new generation' of royals are taking on real jobs – often very dangerous and in the public eye. Felipe de Bourbon, crown prince of Spain (heir to the Spanish throne), is a trained military helicopter pilot.

VOICE OF THE PEOPLE

SHARED EMOTIONS
It is easy to forget that privileged royals suffer some of the same joys and pain of other people. In 2009, Britain's Prince William became royal patron of the Child Bereavement Charity, which his mother (Diana, Princess of Wales) had supported. Her death in 1997 had left William and his brother Harry devastated: 'Never being able to say the word "mummy" again in your life sounds like a small thing. However, for many, including me, it's now really just a word – hollow and evoking memories.'

TIMELINE... TIMELINE... TIMELINE... TIMELINE... TIMELINE... TIMELINE...

1814 CE   Norwegian and Swedish monarchies unite

On-the-job training

A childhood growing up in a royal household might seem full of advantages, with travel, wealth and people ready to run all sorts of errands. But it is also very limiting. Imagine never being able to jump on a bike and ride to a friend's house or to decide on the spur of the moment to go to a café or a film. The need for security means that all royals are watched over constantly.

As well as being watched, young members of a royal family begin to accompany their parents at public functions: opening museums and schools, watching awards ceremonies, visiting schools and hospitals, and so on. In a typical year, there might be almost 400 of those functions. If a prince or princess has begun attending them from the age of 12, he or she will be very experienced when the time comes to inherit the throne.

The question of how – and when – to prepare for the role as a monarch is very tricky in the modern world (see The voting booth). Removing young royals from official duties to give them more life experience also runs the risk of leaving them unprepared when the time comes to assume royal duties.

THE VOTING BOOTH

How to prepare?

In addition to showing that they have had the right experience to govern, political leaders are often criticized for being out of touch with ordinary voters, or the real world. Unlike politicians of 40 or 50 years ago (who might have run companies, worked in mines or been soldiers before entering politics), modern politicians have usually spent their entire adulthood living and breathing politics.

Do you think that the same accusation – of being out of touch – is true of a country's royal family? Can you think of some way in which royals could share more of the experiences of their subjects? Or do they do enough already?

TIMELINE... TIMELINE... TIMELINE... TIMELINE... TIMELINE... TIMELINE...

1861 Kingdom of Italy established	1871 German Empire established, with Prussia at its core

End of the line

If people are unhappy with their prime minister or president, voters can remove them at the next election. Democratic government remains, but the new leader (or governing party) can still make sweeping changes. Replacing a king or queen is a different matter: it is more common to get rid of an entire monarchy than to replace a reigning monarch.

VOICE OF THE PEOPLE

EXECUTING THE ROMANOVS

The execution of the Russian royal family (the Romanovs) on 17 July 1918 followed a brutal logic. The new communist government, which had seized power during the revolution, knew that Tsar Nicholas II and his family were symbols of the monarchy. The country was in the middle of a civil war and pro-monarchy forces were trying to rescue the Romanovs. The communists wanted to make sure the monarchy could not be restored if they were defeated.

By mid-July 1918, the Romanovs had been moved to Ekaterinburg, thousands of kilometres away from Russia's main cities. As pro-monarchy forces closed in on Ekaterinburg, the government decided to execute the royal family and dispose of their bodies. Pavel Medvedev was a member of the squad of soldiers who were guarding the Romanovs. He later described how the royal family entered the room where they would soon be shot: 'The maid carried a pillow. The tsar's daughters also brought small pillows with them. One pillow was put on the empress's chair; another on the heir's chair. It seemed as if all of them guessed their fate, but not one of them uttered a single sound. At this moment eleven men entered the room: Yurovsky [head of the execution squad], his assistant, two members of the Extraordinary Commission [local revolutionary government], and seven [secret police].'

An elderly Russian holds an icon (sacred image) of Nicholas II, Russia's last tsar. Many Russians believe that Nicholas, who was murdered during the Russian Revolution, is a saint.

Off with their heads

Political revolutions have overthrown many monarchies over the centuries, even though some countries later reversed their actions. Representatives of the English parliament executed King Charles I during the Civil War, Louis XVI and his wife Marie-Antoinette were victims of the French Revolution and Tsar Nicholas II and his entire family were shot during the Russian Revolution.

In these cases, anti-monarchy forces realized how powerful a symbol a living king or queen (or tsar) could be. In less chaotic circumstances, once-powerful monarchs can live out their lives in comfort. In 1918, **Kaiser** Wilhelm II fled to the Netherlands when revolution was about to overthrow the German monarchy. Dutch Queen Wilhelmina

TIMELINE... TIMELINE... TIMELINE... TIMELINE... TIMELINE... TIMELINE...

| 1918 | Austro-Hungarian kingdom, German Empire abolished | 1931 | Spanish monarchy overthrown |

Norodom Sihanouk offers up a prayer at the Silver Pagoda in Phnom Penh, Cambodia's capital, shortly after his return from 13 years' exile in 1991.

refused to expel him (to face trial for **war crimes**), and the former kaiser bought a mansion, where he lived until his death in 1941. Soon after Wilhelm's exile, however, the German government allowed him back into the country to collect his things. He returned to the Netherlands with more than two dozen railway cars full of belongings – including a car and a boat.

TIMELINE... TIMELINE... TIMELINE... TIMELINE... TIMELINE... TIMELINE

| 1938 CE | British King Edward VIII abdicates | 1970 | Cambodian monarchy overthrown |

RETURN OF THE KING

The German political philosopher Karl Marx (1818–1883) and his followers (known as Marxists) believed that human history was predictable. Marx argued that change took place because of a constant struggle between social **classes** to gain power. Capitalism (the system that encourages individuals to set up their own businesses) took over from the **feudalism** of the Middle Ages because the rising merchant class wanted the freedom to go into business. In Marx's view, capitalism would eventually fall apart as the working class (which produced the goods) gained power.

According to this view, the idea of monarchy was becoming outdated by the time feudalism developed in the ninth century. By the twentieth century Marx predicted that **communism** would replace capitalism. Imagine the surprise of Marxist political experts when countries turn back to monarchies, despite having got rid of their kings and queens earlier.

Britain restored its monarchy in 1660 after civil war and eleven years of parliamentary rule. But the new king, Charles II, was aware that he had returned 'by popular request' and so needed to respect British public opinion. Just over 25 years later, the British welcomed another king (William III) from the Netherlands. However, the strict controls over the monarchy that Parliament put in place in 1688 drastically reduced the king's political power.

In the late twentieth century, two other countries – which had also suffered terrible civil wars – turned back to their monarchies as a way of healing national wounds. Spain's civil war in the 1930s led to more than three decades of military dictatorship under General Franco. The country welcomed King Juan Carlos back in 1975, when Franco died. Cambodia had an even more turbulent period during the 1970s, when the Khmer Rouge (an extremist communist government) murdered millions of civilians. Norodom Sihanouk was returned to the Cambodian throne to preside over a constitutional monarchy when the Khmer Rouge leaders were driven from the country.

TIMELINE... TIMELINE... TIMELINE... TIMELINE... TIMELINE... TIMELINE...

| 1975 | Spanish monarchy restored | 1993 | Cambodian monarchy restored |

Monarchy and the media

On 29 April 2011, thousands of couples celebrated their marriages on a warm spring day in Great Britain. The happy events would be captured on smart phones and digital cameras, but the world's attention was focused on just one of those weddings. Prince William, second in line to the British throne (after his father, Prince Charles), was marrying Catherine Middleton, who he had met while studying at Saint Andrew's University in Scotland.

The 2011 royal wedding had an enormous audience, watched in some form by people in 180 countries. Like a previous 'family wedding' – when Prince Charles married Lady Diana Spencer

Princess Charlotte makes her first appearance on the Buckingham Palace balcony in June 2016 – four generations of British royalty were assembled.

PUBLIC RELATIONS

Image – how the public views a person or organization – is an important feature of modern politics. Skilled politicians can make sure that voters learn about any news story that makes them look good – consoling victims of disasters, being present when a national sportsperson wins a world championship, and so on. They use a technique called **spin** to play down stories that are less favourable to them.

These are examples of public relations (or PR). Monarchies depend as much as elected governments on PR, and their success is often measured in terms of how the public reacts. Prince Edward's celebrity television programme was bad PR, just as the royal divorces of Prince Charles, Prince Andrew and Princess Anne had been.

More recently, Britain's royal family has improved its PR in an area that is important to many taxpayers – money. Since 1993, the queen has paid income tax in the same way as everyone else in Britain and other royals have published much clearer accounts of how they spend their money.

in 1981 – it captivated millions of people around world. The media played an important role in making this possible, devoting hours of coverage to the preparations, ceremony and celebrations afterwards.

Communications technology had moved on dramatically in the intervening thirty years. People commented on the proceedings as they took place, using Facebook, Twitter and other social media. YouTube reported that the 'William-Kate' wedding had the highest-ever number of live streams (72 million) of any single event.

People seem to love to watch or read about royal weddings, and the media profit from that interest. One of the first televised royal weddings had been a media landmark of the 1950s. Prince Rainier of the Monaco married American film star Grace Kelly in 1956. The world was dazzled by the glamour of the lavish ceremony. Other weddings involving members of the Japanese, Dutch and Spanish royal families maintained that interest – and boosted the image of monarchies in general.

Public opinion

It came as no surprise that the 1981 royal wedding in Britain received such uncritical acclaim. The British monarchy had a handsome young prince marrying a beautiful woman, and the couple seemed to combine traditional and modern values. But public opinion can change, and the media is quick to capture that change of mood.

Queen Elizabeth II referred to the year 1992 as an 'annus horribilis' (Latin for horrible year). In the same year, her daughter Princess Anne was divorced, her son Prince Andrew separated from his wife, and a 'tell-all' book revealed splits in the Charles-Diana marriage. Scandals in other royal families made the public view the institution of monarchy itself more critically. Action needed to be taken.

British people sometimes refer to their royal family as 'The Firm' because of its huge size and influence. Like any major company, it has a management structure and someone sitting firmly at the top (the reigning monarch). Like modern companies, it has become aware of the image it presents to the outside world. Many people believe that the new generation of royalty (William, Kate and their family) will help restore some of the royal family's timeless attraction (typified by Queen Elizabeth's Diamond Jubilee in 2012).

TWENTY-FIRST CENTURY BATTLE-LINES

People have been arguing for and against monarchies for centuries, so it shouldn't be surprising that many of the fiercest arguments are now conducted on the Internet – through blogs, on official websites (both pro- and anti-monarchy), and through social networking sites such as Twitter. In November 2010, Queen Elizabeth II joined Facebook, but with some alterations – users are unable to 'poke' or to send her 'friend requests'.

THE VOTING BOOTH

The royals – fair game?

Many people believe that reporters and celebrity photographers (known as paparazzi) go too far in their coverage of Britain's royal family. They argue that the royals have less privacy than ordinary individuals and some even believe that the persistence of these photographers led to the car crash in which Princess Diana died in 1997.

Others believe that if taxpayers fund the royal family's travel, palaces and extravagant lifestyle they should be informed about how their money is spent – especially during troubled economic times when so many ordinary people are struggling. Do you think that the media interferes with the royals too much?

The wreckage of the car in which Princess Diana died is pulled from the tunnel in Paris where it crashed at high speed.

Looking ahead

People have predicted the end of monarchies for 2,500 years, since the Romans replaced their monarchy with a republic, and yet they still survive in the twenty-first century. Few monarchs wield real power, but monarchies provide many people with a comforting sense of tradition and order, which might be the key to their survival.

MEASURING MONARCHIES?

Is the idea of maintaining a monarchy – with the palaces and pageantry – a waste of money in tough economic times? Monarchists refer to the Legatum Institute, an international organization which 'researches and promotes the principles that drive the creation of global prosperity and the expansion of human liberty'. Every year it examines the factors that allow countries to become prosperous, with happy inhabitants. They include health, safety and security, education and personal freedom. Below is a list of the top 15 countries in the 2015 list (based on a combination of all the factors listed above).

1 *Norway*
2 Switzerland
3 *Denmark*
4 *New Zealand*
5 *Sweden*
6 *Canada*
7 *Australia*
8 *Netherlands*
9 Finland
10 Ireland
11 United States
12 Iceland
13 Luxembourg
14 Germany
15 *United Kingdom*

More than half these countries – the ones in *italics* – are monarchies. Seven of the top ten and four of the top five countries are monarchies. It seems that even in an age of cuts and penny-pinching, monarchies are providing good value for money.

VOICE OF THE PEOPLE

CITIZENS' VIEWS
This contribution to a website called the Commonwealth conversation is from Massachusetts, and a supporter of monarchy: 'I look at my citizens today in the world's banner republic, and I see no traditions. I see a vast horde easily swayed by fear. I see not men but livestock. Republics degenerate into mob rule. Seriously, look at our presidents; I'd not fight or die for any of them over the past 20 years! But for a monarch, a not partisan figure who represents all that is good and honourable about one's country, I'd gladly go to war!'

On the other hand, one of Britain's best-loved cookery writers, Delia Smith, wrote in The Times *in 2009: 'I'm not anti the queen. But monarchy in general, I can't see the point. Because I believe everybody is equal, I can't believe in having to walk backwards… What I do believe in is leadership.'*

Lord Irvine, a senior Cabinet member, bows to Queen Elizabeth at an official function in 2000. Will such a gesture seem outdated in 25 years time?

Glossary

abdicate   To formally give up royal duties.

absolute monarch   A monarch who has complete political power over a country.

Austro-Hungarian Empire   An empire that combined the monarchies of Austria and Hungary from 1867 to 1918.

bill   The wording of a new law presented to a law-making body such as Parliament for approval.

carbuncle   A large and unattractive swelling under the skin.

citizen   A member of a society in which everyone has the same rights and duties and no one has special privileges.

Civil List   The annual amount of money that Parliament gives to the British royal family and royal household.

class   A group of people, such as merchants or nobles, sharing a social or economic position.

College of Cardinals   The group of cardinals (most senior clergy) of the Catholic Church which elects a new pope after the death of the previous pope.

Commonwealth of Nations   An international organization of 54 independent countries (most of which were once ruled by Britain) which work together to promote peaceful development.

communism   A political system in which all property is owned by the community and each person contributes and receives according to their ability and needs. A communist government provides work, health care, education and housing, but may deny people certain freedoms.

compromise   The settlement of a dispute in which each side gives ground to the other.

Congress   The elected law-making body of the United States, consisting of the House of Representatives and the Senate.

constitutional monarchy   A form of government in which the monarch acts as head of state, but elected officials have political power.

democracy   A form of government in which people choose political leaders by voting.

dynasty   A series of rulers from the same family.

emir   An independent ruler of a Muslim country.

feudalism   A system of government in which nobles gave people land and protection; in return, they had to work and fight for the noble.

First World War   The war fought mainly in Europe between 1914 and 1918.

free press   The legal right of newspapers, television, radio and other communicators to report events without government control.

governor-general   An appointed representative of the British monarch in a country that recognizes the monarch as its head of state.

head of state   The person who represents the state (or nation) in public affairs.

heredity (in monarchies)   Passing power from parent to child, or to another relative, when a monarch dies.